AF488455

ISBN: 9798218324520

Legal Disclaimer:

The information contained in this book represents the author's personal opinions and does not constitute formal or legal advice intended to prevent accidents or injuries. Skateboarding and other wheel sports are hazardous activities with inherent safety risks. Always consult the official rules sign posted by the operator of the skatepark. The author assumes no responsibility or liability for loss or damages resulting from the use of information contained herein.

THE
SKATEPARK ETIQUETTE
GUIDE

12 ESSENTIAL TIPS FOR A SMOOTH SKATEPARK EXPERIENCE

VINCE ONEL

ILLUSTRATED BY TODD BRATRUD

DEDICATED TO MY BOYS
OLIVER + ALEXANDER

SKATEPARKS ARE MAGICAL LANDSCAPES WITH LIMITLESS POSSIBILITIES.

Unique spaces where you can progress your skills, conquer your fears and most importantly, feel a sense of community and belonging.

To a beginner making their first trip to the skatepark though, the environment can feel chaotic and intimidating. And for more advanced riders, sharing space with someone who doesn't understand the unwritten rules of the skatepark can negatively impact safety and functionality.

That's why I've created this guide.

Informed beginners create a more enjoyable experience for all.

While this guide won't prevent all conflicts and uncomfortable situations, it will give you the confidence and baseline understanding of skatepark mechanics to spend more time enjoying yourself and less time feeling unsure.

Skateparks are certainly chaotic, but there is an order and organization to the chaos. And in the heart of that chaos awaits a whole lot of fun!

12 ESSENTIAL TIPS

1. WAIT YOUR TURN
2. WAIT AT THE EDGES
3. GO WITH THE FLOW
4. AVOID TAILGATING
5. BOARD!
6. KEEP YOUR EYES + EARS OPEN
7. DON'T BE A COPYCAT
8. WAX WITH CAUTION
9. PRACTICE CLEANLINESS
10. EARLY BIRD GETS THE WORM
11. GAMES OF S.K.A.T.E.
12. HAVE FUN!

THE GOLDEN RULE OF SKATEPARK ETIQUETTE.

You've decided it's time to start your run – now what? Rather than impulsively pushing off, you'll first want to look around and assess the active traffic around you.

Just like you learned to look both ways before crossing the street, the same logic applies at skateparks.

Once you've looked around and determined there's enough of an opening in the traffic to safely blend in with the rest of the riders, go for it!

You may also notice an informal queue of sorts has formed where "skateboarder A" goes, while "skateboarder B" and "skateboarder C" wait their turn. When there's enough separation and open space to avoid collisions, "skateboarder B" goes and the cycle naturally continues. Figure out where you land in the queue and try to follow that order the best that you can.

There won't always be a clear order and the order may change over time, but pay attention and you should be able to pick it up.

Now if you don't wait your turn and abruptly cut off other riders already in motion, you'll start to hear the term "snake" thrown around.

A skatepark full of snakes who don't wait their turn is pure chaos and no fun. You'll spend less time blasting big airs and more time nursing collision injuries. So don't be a snake.

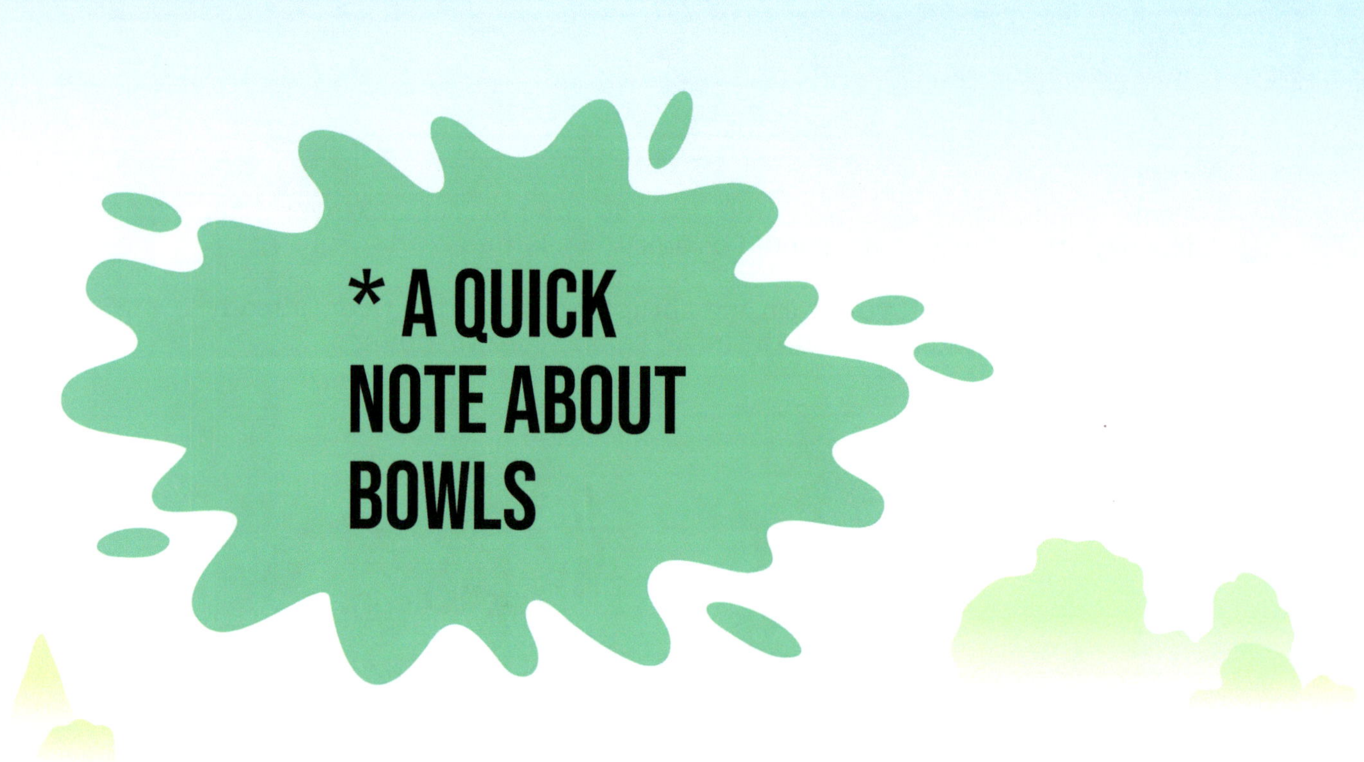

BOWLS ARE UNIQUE OBSTACLES WITHIN THE SKATEPARK UNIVERSE.

While the principle of waiting your turn generally applies in the same way when riding a bowl, there are a few differences that are worth mentioning.

In contrast to more street-focused terrain which can accommodate multiple riders at a given time, a bowl can typically be used by only one rider at a time. Unless it's a large, expansive bowl with multiple sections, be prepared to be a little more patient when waiting your turn.

It's also smart to assume a longer lead time when waiting for a bowl because bowl runs typically last longer. For the most part, street-focused terrain is the site of quick single tricks or long runs that are linear in nature. Bowl runs on the other hand are contained in a more compact and circular area. Thus, it's not uncommon for a single run to last a full minute, if not more.

MULTIPLE RIDERS CAN SIMULTANEOUSLY UTILIZE A PUMP TRACK.

Unlike the majority of bowls which can be used by only one rider at a time, the linear nature of a pump track allows multiple riders to simultaneously utilize a track.

If you're a more cautious rider, you may prefer to wait until someone fully completes their run, but since it's possible that a rider may loop the track multiple times, it's perfectly acceptable to enter a track already in use by another rider. Just wait at least a couple seconds and make sure you leave the existing rider enough buffer space to avoid collisions.

A chairlift is a helpful analogy. Multiple snowboarders can ride up the lift at a single time, but the chairs are spaced apart so that when you're ready to dismount there's enough time and space to minimize collisions.

Many pump track layouts feature a designated flat area where riders can queue up, so it should be clear where to wait. These areas often include painted directional arrows, so when your turn is up, your entry and exit points should be clear as well.

2. WAIT AT THE EDGES

THERE'S A RIGHT AND WRONG PLACE TO WAIT.

When your turn is over, either by completing a trick, a series of tricks in a line or failing to land a trick, it's time to swiftly move out of the way and allow other riders space for their turn. Obviously if you are seriously injured, take your time and ask for help as necessary.

Rather than waiting in the middle of the skatepark or next to your most recent obstacle, it's best to clear out to the perimeter edges of the skatepark, which are typically flat. You don't need to stand all the way out in the landscape beyond the skatepark, but the more space you allow others while waiting, the better.

In addition to the position of your feet and body, it's important to pay attention to the location of your skateboard and make sure it's out of the way as well. Especially at the edges of a bowl, when the board of a rider waiting their turn is too close to the lip, it can create a mental distraction and possibly lead to collisions.

THERE'S A RIGHT AND WRONG PLACE TO WATCH.

Family, friends and curious pedestrians are all welcome to watch the captivating theatre skateparks have to offer.

Primary areas for watching are typically located adjacent to the skatepark's entry points, where pathways provide connection from a parking lot. Designers strategically locate these areas at entry points so that spectators can access seating and clear vantage points without having to traverse through active skatepark terrain where high-speed skateboarding creates a significant risk of collisions.

It's important that both non-skateboarders and skateboarders who want to take a break do not sit on obstacles within the skatepark. Not sure if what you're hoping to sit on is a skatepark obstacle? If the edges are marked by wax and paint scuffs, it's likely an obstacle a skateboarder will want to utilize in the near future. If not, it's likely a pedestrian bench and you're good to go.

Some skateparks supplement a primary seating area at the entrance with additional spectator areas within the heart of the skatepark terrain itself. If you'd like to access those areas, walk cautiously and cede the right-of-way to active skateboarders.

3. GO WITH THE FLOW

THE COMMUNITY IS YOUR COMPASS.

Understanding the primary flow pattern of a skatepark is extremely important for beginners.

When you first arrive at the skatepark, spend some time watching the action before you start riding yourself. This allows you to safely develop a sense for how riders are moving through the space, without learning the hard way by crashing into someone.

A primary flow pattern forms naturally at most skateparks, typically oriented around the skatepark's longest direction. For example, if your skatepark is 60' wide in the east-west direction and 200' wide in the north-south direction, the most common traffic flow will be in the north-south direction. So in order to blend in with the collectively agreed upon flow, you'll want to ride either in line with other riders or parallel to them in the north-south direction.

What you don't want to do is ride perpendicular to the main current. If the majority of riders are flowing north-south and you ride in the east-west direction, you're creating eyeline blind spots and setting yourself up for "T bone" collisions.

For example, if someone is riding back and forth in a mini half-pipe, it's a major faux pas to ride through the middle of the mini's flat bottom.

4. AVOID TAILGATING

MAINTAIN A HEALTHY DISTANCE.

Tailgating is a term borrowed from vehicular traffic. In essence, tailgating means following someone too closely. When you "tailgate" someone at a skatepark, you're following them so closely that if they stop or miss their trick, you have not left sufficient distance to stop yourself without crashing into them.

It's also important not to tailgate because feeling someone's presence too close to you is mentally distracting, potentially causing you to lose focus on the trick you're performing.

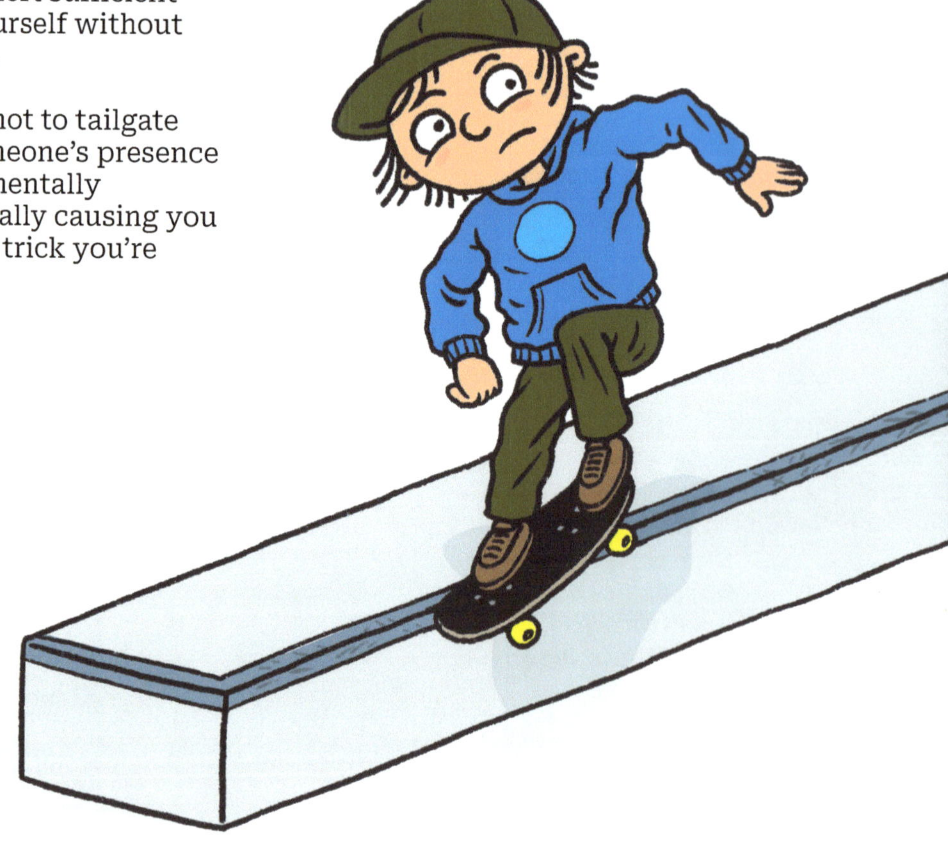

If the person in front of you lands their trick and keeps moving forward, great, but even the best skateboarders miss from time to time, so a spacious buffer is critical in those moments.

5. BOARD!

FIND YOUR VOICE.

Throughout a typical day at the skatepark, there will be multiple instances where a rider unsuccessfully attempts a trick and their skateboard shoots out at a high speed away from them. Hopefully the runaway skateboard naturally loses steam without hitting anyone.

And hopefully other riders are able to see the skateboard coming before it disrupts their run. In reality though, skateboarders often have tunnel vision and are so focused on the trick they're performing, that they don't see a loose skateboard coming toward them.

The exact origins are debated, but a now commonly held practice at skateparks is to yell "BOARD!" when a skateboard gets loose and a collision is possible. Yelling "BOARD!" is essentially the same as saying "watch out". It's just more specific and familiar to the ears of a seasoned skateboarder who then knows exactly how to react.

Typically you'd use this technique when it's your own board that's gotten away from you, but it's totally acceptable to shout the word when someone else's board is wildly darting through the skatepark.

Also, keep in mind that many skateboarders wear headphones, so don't be shy with your voice when alerting the rest of the skatepark to the situation.

Whether it's preventing an ankle injury or giving someone a heads up that allows them to stop a skateboard before it hits a hard edge and chips the wood, this generational principle is beneficial for all.

6. KEEP YOUR EYES + EARS OPEN

BE ALERT. BE AWARE.

Skateboarding is highly technical and can require intense concentration, so it's very common to slip into "tunnel vision" when riding at a skatepark. It's important to remember though, that you are sharing a community space with others, so it's respectful to remain present and be aware of your surroundings by keeping your eyes and ears open at all times.

Use your eyes to continually scan the skatepark as close to 360 degrees as possible and you will give yourself more time to preempt collisions – either by swerving out of the way or flowing to a less crowded area.

Headphones are commonly used at skateparks, but try to avoid turning up the volume too loud. If you can't hear anything other than your music, you'll miss a fellow rider warning you about a runway board, notifying you about a rail that's extra slick from yesterday's wax or requesting that you temporarily move away from an obstacle so they can attempt a trick.

Music can definitely be motivating and therapeutic, but over-use of headphones can isolate you from the communal energy of a skatepark. Connecting with others is one of the most rewarding aspects of skateparks, so do your best to find the right balance.

7. DON'T BE A COPYCAT

BE AN INDIVIDUAL. NOT AN IMITATOR.

Skateboard tricks do not come easy. They require significant persistence, dedication and fortitude.

If you see someone at the skatepark struggling with a trick or skill that you mastered long ago, be sympathetic to their struggle and do not attempt that same trick. No one likes a showoff, so rather than trying to embarrass that person by demonstrating how easy the trick is for you, take the higher, more humble road and shift your focus to a different trick.

There are hundreds, if not thousands, of skateboard trick possibilities, so finding another trick shouldn't be hard. Plus, the essence of skateboarding is about expressing your individual personality and creativity. It's not a showboating competition.

And if you really want to try that same trick and can't wait until the other rider has moved on, feel free to ask them if they mind. Who knows, they may have no issue with it or even welcome the motivation.

A HEADS UP GOES A LONG WAY.

Typically purchased at your local skateboard shop, wax acts as a lubricant when grinds / slides on skatepark obstacles are meeting too much resistance.

The amount of wax you apply is definitely a matter of personal preference. Some old school purists will refuse wax and say "just go faster", while others like a ledge to glide like butter.

If you're sessioning an obstacle with multiple people and feel like it needs
some wax, first ask your session buddies if they're cool with it. More than
likely they'll say they don't mind or make a friendly suggestion on the wax
amount they prefer.

The important thing you've done is given others a heads up that the
obstacle is now waxy. This allows them to prepare speed and force
accordingly, instead of being surprised when they land on the obstacle
and it's too late to avoid a wipe out.

If no one's at the skatepark, wax away, but be considerate of riders coming
later in the day who may have different wax preferences and would prefer
not to be surprised.

9. PRACTICE CLEANLINESS

RESPECT YOUR SKATEPARK.

This tip is just common sense. And realistically applies to respecting any shared public space.

Most public skateparks are maintained by a local municipality that regularly handles trash removal and general upkeep. But the frequency and quality of that maintenance can vary, so day-to-day cleanliness is in the hands of riders.

It should go without saying, but just in case it's not clear, graffiti is a major no no. It can lead to the skatepark getting shut down. It can make the skatepark surface dangerously slick or conversely, when the municipality is forced to remove it with harsh techniques, the resulting surface can be very rough.

Hydration is obviously encouraged, so drinks are perfectly acceptable, but ideally you're consuming liquids within spectator or non-skateable gathering areas, just in case there's a spill. When you finish a drink, toss it in the nearest recycling or trash receptacle. Don't just leave it for someone else to deal with.

Food is typically discouraged at the skatepark because it's so messy and can create tripping hazards when spilled. So ideally wait until after your session to eat, but if you absolutely have to, consume your food as far away from active riding areas as possible.

10. EARLY BIRD GETS THE WORM

LEARN YOUR SKATEPARK'S PEAK HOURS.

A skatepark at peak hours packed with skateboarders and other wheel sports athletes can be intimidating for a beginner hoping to ease into things. By and large, skateparks are friendly environments, but it's not hard to imagine that as a skatepark gets busier, the risk of collisions and stressful situations increases.

Wrapping your head around both skateboarding itself and the various tips detailed in this guide will be a whole lot easier when the skatepark is less busy. To give yourself the highest odds of a sparsely populated skatepark, it's best to visit the skatepark early in the morning. That commonly means sometime between sunrise and 10 a.m.. And even better if that's during the week, when skateparks are generally less crowded.

During the week, peak hours are typically from 3 p.m. to 7 p.m..

During the weekend, peak hours are typically from 11 a.m. to 8 p.m..

If your local skatepark has lights for nighttime use, that may impact the timing of peak hours, but the general rule of thumb is that skateparks get more crowded as the day goes on.

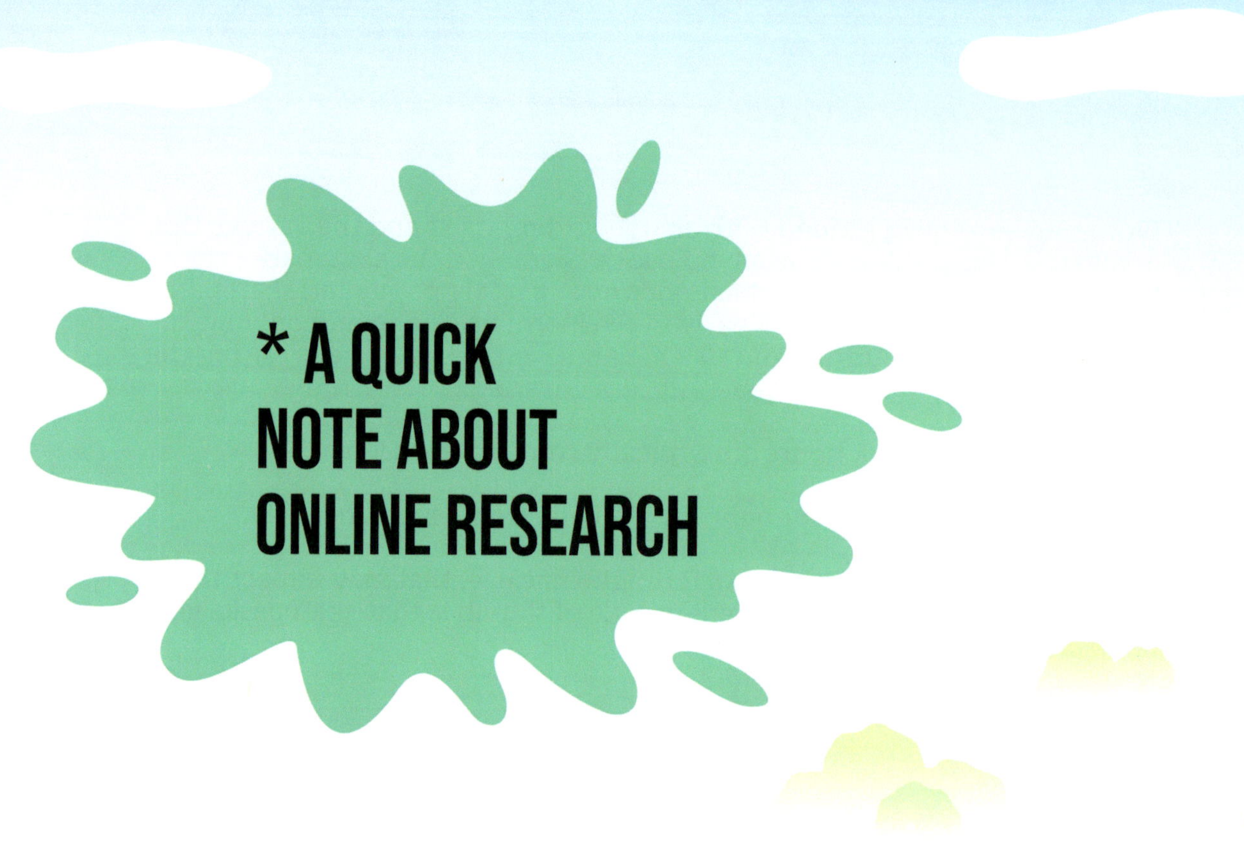

ADDITIONAL INFO IS AT YOUR FINGERTIPS.

While many skateparks are not fenced and freely open from dawn to dusk, some skateparks are operated more strictly with a lockable gate, specific hours and other various rules. If you're the type of person who feels most comfortable when you're over-prepared, feel free to do some online research to better understand the various requirements and available amenities of the skatepark you plan on visiting.

The local municipality's website may have a sub-page dedicated to the skatepark or you can visit one of the many skatepark directory websites out there, which in general are fairly accurate and feature a lot of insightful photographs.

11. GAMES OF S.K.A.T.E.

SKATEBOARDING'S VERSION OF H.O.R.S.E.

S.K.A.T.E. is a friendly competition based on the well-known game of H.O.R.S.E. from basketball.

The game typically involves 2 players, but in theory, there's no limit to the number of players. The main focus is on flat ground tricks, but it can expand to a specific obstacle or you can even make the entire skatepark fair game for tricks.

Rock paper scissors or some other method determines who goes first. The first player then attempts a trick. If they land that trick, the second player must successfully execute that trick or receive an "S". If the first player doesn't land their trick, it's the second player's turn to attempt a trick of their choosing.

The players then go back and forth challenging each other to match tricks, receiving letters in the S.K.A.T.E. sequence until one person fails to replicate five tricks and is declared the loser.

Other than keeping in mind that you shouldn't get too aggressively competitive, the primary etiquette related to S.K.A.T.E. is that the game should be played off to the side – not in the middle of the skatepark. Learn the flow of the skatepark and find a flat area where you can play without disrupting other riders. These games can last as long as 30 minutes, so finding the right spot ensures your game isn't interrupted.

POSITIVE ENERGY IS CONTAGIOUS.

Progression and competition are inherent aspects of skateboarding and there can be tense moments at the skatepark when someone is attempting a precarious or highly technical maneuver, but at its core, the spirit of skateboarding is about having fun.

Skateboarding is not a traditional team sport with strict regulations and point scoring systems, so don't take yourself too seriously. A positive and light-hearted mindset is contagious and will spread throughout the skatepark, creating the perfect energy for a great session.

When someone is struggling with a trick, lift them up with words of encouragement. And when they finally win the battle, celebrate their accomplishment with high fives and cheers.

Skateparks reach their full potential when they transcend beyond basic recreational facility and become a vibrant community gathering space where social bonds form and grow. Focus on having fun and you'll be amazed by the special connections you'll make at your new "home".

SKATEPARK

An area specifically designated for skateboarding and other wheel sports, typically consisting of concrete obstacles, and typically operated by a municipality

SKATE SPOT

A scaled-down version of a skatepark, with just a handful of elements, typically intended to accommodate a small number of riders

PUMP TRACK

A series of rhythmic pathways made up of rollers and bermed turns, typically constructed with concrete, asphalt or compacted earth

BOWL

A curvilinear concrete basin emulating the empty backyard swimming pools that revolutionized skateboarding

STREET PLAZA

A type of skatepark that shifts the focus away from traditional ramps and bowls, toward elements of urban architecture such as steps, railings and walls

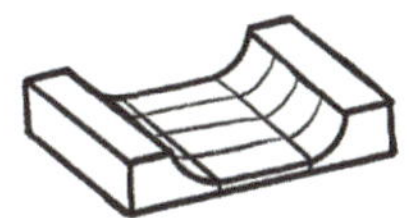

MINI HALF-PIPE

Opposing quarter-pipes arranged in a parallel layout to create ½ of a full circle or "pipe"

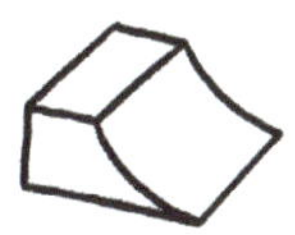

QUARTER-PIPE

A radiused ramp creating ¼ of a full circle or "pipe"

COPING

The steel pipe lining the top of a quarter-pipe

OLLIE

A maneuver that pops the skateboard off the ground, allowing the rider to "jump" over and onto obstacles

GOOFY

One of two options for skateboard foot position. When pushing to generate momentum, goofy riders' right foot stays on the front of the board, while the left pushes off the ground.

REGULAR

One of two options for skateboard foot position. When pushing to generate momentum, regular riders' left foot stays on the front of the board, while the right pushes off the ground.

Vince Onel is a husband, father of two young boys and avid skateboarder of 25+ years.

In his professional life, he is Co-Owner and Design Director at Spohn Ranch – the Los Angeles based skatepark design-build firm responsible for hundreds of critically-acclaimed municipal skateparks across the country.

Over the course of three decades, Vince has ridden thousands of skateparks and personally designed hundreds of them. Countless hours spent analyzing skateboard flow patterns and riding concrete of all shapes and sizes has given Vince a uniquely intimate understanding of skatepark mechanics. That in-depth knowledge and a passion for educating youth skateboarders inspired The Skatepark Etiquette Guide.

Photos: Michael Stanfield

Todd Bratrud is one of the skateboarding world's most prolific and iconic artists. His skateboarding roots in the small town of Crookston, Minnesota influenced a signature drawing style sought out by many of the industry's premiere brands including Nike, Thrasher Magazine and Birdhouse Skateboards.

Vince and Todd first connected in 2011 when Vince's firm, Spohn Ranch, was hired to design a municipal skatepark in Grand Forks, North Dakota, where Todd was spearheading a grassroots advocacy and fundraising campaign. Their close collaboration that led to Grand Forks' renowned Rydell Skatepark and a shared reverence for skateboarding made Todd the perfect fit to illustrate The Skatepark Etiquette Guide.

Photo: Sam McGuire